# Want It!
# Speak It!

# It's Yours!

by

**Montecia Roulhac**

**Want It Speak It Its Yours**
Montecia Roulhac

**Copyright** © **2017** Montecia Roulhac

ISBN-13: 9781977643636
ISBN-10: 1977643639

All rights reserved. No part of this publication may be reproduced, stored in a retrieval system, or transmitted in any form or by any means, electronic, mechanical, recording or otherwise, without the prior written permission of the author.

Printed in the United States of America.

*Design by* Mariana Vidakovics De Victor

# Acknowledgements

This book is for my children (Alexandria and Sean (SJ)) you can achieve anything you put your mind to, but you must dedicate yourself and immerse yourself. If you do, the world is yours! Mommy loves you guys from the bottom of my heart!

# About Me

I've been in the Human Resources field for 15 years. During that time, I've guided prospective and new employees, as well as the company, with the best strategies to move forward.

I have a passion for helping people reach their professional and personal goals. Unfortunately, trying to reach that next level in your career can be overwhelming. Take heart; I am here to help guide you through that process, so you won't have to do it alone.

I will provide you with various business tools to help you in the process, including resume critique/ edit, job search, social media profile assistance, and so much more.

How can I help you achieve your goals? Besides accumulating 15 years of experience, I earned my Bachelor of Science degree from Alabama State University, as well as an MBA from Keller Graduate School of Management. The focus was in Human Resources.

I have been scouted by companies such Amazon, Google and Salesforce, to name a few.

You may ask where I got my experience? By working for one of the top telecommunication companies in the world. I helped guide individuals of the organization through all stages of the creative process from inception to completion. I coached executives and managers across industries worldwide with significant results. My sole purpose, as your coach, is to guide your life both professionally and personally.

It brings me so much joy to see people I help, accomplish their goals professionally as well as personally. I always believed that if you dedicate yourself to your goals and dreams, you can achieve anything in life!

# Table of Contents

Acknowledgements ................................................................. iii

About Me ................................................................................ iv

Introduction ............................................................................. 1

Step One: How to Let Your Subconscious Mind Be Your Guide ....................................................................................... 3

Step Two: Programming the Subconscious Mind to for Success .................................................................................... 7

Step Three: How to Understand Dreams and Let Them Work for You ......................................................................... 12

Step Four: Learn How to Use Thought So It Will Take You Where You Want to Go ..................................................... 21

Step Five: Understand How Your Feelings Can Control Thoughts for Good or Bad ................................................... 25

Step Six: By Speaking with Power and Conviction You'll Go Far and Be Successful .................................................. 28

Step Seven: How to Believe in Yourself to Achieve What You Want in Life ................................................................ 32

Step Eight: Use Three Methods to Achieve What You Want and Succeed .................................................................. 35

Step Nine: Use This Method to Help You Accomplish Your Goals and Become Successful ....................................... 38

Step Ten: What You Need to Know to Take the Big Step. 42

Step Eleven: Taking Action Means Doing This One Thing ............................................................................................. 46

Step Twelve: Take the Mentality that It's Yours and Let No One Say Differently .................................................................. 54

Getting What You Want by Making Sacrifices ................... 58

Are You Prepared for What You Want? ............................. 60

Wrap Up .................................................................................. 62

## Introduction

Before I get started, I'd like to introduce to you a young woman. Her name is Alex. Her long-range goal is to start a chain of restaurants. She daydreams about it. The problem for her is her thinking. She thinks it may not be possible. She doubts herself, even though she sees it happening sometime down the road.

Do you think that way? Do you think about something you want to achieve, but doubt you will have it? Self-doubt is not new. Many people think about and dream about starting their own business, climbing the tallest mountain, swimming the deepest, sea, and so on. What keeps them from accomplishing their goals and desires? It's self-doubt.

Self-doubt can leave to self-sabotage. You think about something you can do, but previous self-defeating programming surfaces and forces you to go in another direction with your thoughts. The result – you fail to achieve what you want. You feel like a loser. Sometimes, you may end up feeling depressed.

## Want It! Speak It! It's Yours!

There is a way to turn your attitude around and become a winner. All it takes is to follow certain steps that lead to what you desire the most: Want It, Speak It, and It's Yours.

Alex got turned around and I am going to tell you how I helped her. By following my advice, you too can achieve an amazing life. It takes one step and you'll be on your way.

Are you ready to take that step? It's more than one step. I will provide for you several steps that will guide you in the right direction toward your journey of self-discovery.

*Are you ready?...*
*Let's Go!...*

## [Step One]

## How to Let Your Subconscious Mind

## Be Your Guide

Do you want it! Do you really want it! Are you so anxious and excited for it that you are willing to do what it takes to get it? If this is how you feel, you are off to a good start. Just dreaming something doesn't necessarily mean you will achieve it. You must want to accomplish it.

Someone once said you must live and breathe it to know you want it. I agree with that. You must want it so ingrained in you that you will take whatever risks are necessary to get the goal you dreamt of doing. You'll say that it is not an easy feat. No, some steps will be hard. Some will be easy. Since when is life fair. However, if you develop the attitude that you can do it, you're on your way to success.

## Want It! Speak It! It's Yours!

How does one do it? How does one get what they want? How does one achieve what they dream about? It all starts with your thoughts and the subconscious mind. Let me explain.

Before we get into dreams, let me explain to you how the subconscious mind works. The subconscious mind controls your behavior, thereby shaping your personality. Unlike the conscious mind that contains thoughts you are aware of, the subconscious contains thoughts that are not consciously aware of, at least at any given moment.

For example, if you have a fear of eating chicken, you may have an unconscious belief that eating chickens is wrong. Or you saw a chicken get killed, and that hurt you so badly, that it stuck in your subconscious mind. So, when you see a chicken, you avoid it. You won't be aware of it, as your subconscious mind takes over and feeds your conscious the information. Consciously, you fear touching it.

Here's another example of how the subconscious mind works. If you are afraid to act on a dream, it could be that you lack self-confidence. Where did that come from? Certain negative beliefs you received about yourself when younger. This belief causes you to doubt yourself and think you can't do it.

Let's look at the subconscious mind. It's like computer RAM (Random Access Memory). For those who don't know what RAM is, just know it is a place where software is stored when it runs. The subconscious mind stores your beliefs, memories, and life experiences. Everything you absorb from your five senses goes into your conscious for processing, and then to your subconscious for storage until needed.

Look at it another way. The subconscious mind works by one rule: "You get what you focus on." If you received a false or negative belief, you'll focus on that and end up on the short end of the stick. On the other hand, if you received a positive or true belief, you'd focus on that which drives you to be successful.

How can you train your subconscious mind to work for you? The next step will explain how.

Want It! Speak It! It's Yours!

## Points to Ponder

These are questions you won't be graded on or required to answer. They are here simply for reflection and help you to remember more of what you read.

1. What have you learned regarding the subconscious mind?

2. What are two reasons the subconscious mind is useful for you?

3. Will you use your subconscious mind to better yourself and achieve your goals?

## [Step Two]

# Programming the Subconscious Mind to for Success

Based on step one, you know the subconscious mind is what controls how you live your life.

The question is, how can you have it control you the right way?

There are certain rules you must follow for the subconscious mind to work for you.

## Rule 1: You must know what you want first

Before you even take a step, you must know what it is you want to feed your subconscious. This is paramount. Feeding it with the wrong information will lead to problems for you.

You must be specific as to what you want. Just be rational about your choice. After all, don't suggest you want to be Superman. It won't work.

Keep your mind focused on one thing at a time. If you try to focus on more than one thing, you are going to confuse yourself and end up at a dead end.

## Rule 2: Find the patterns that are stopping you from progressing

Everyone, no matter who he/she is, has deep inner beliefs that are keeping him/her from achieving success in life. The best way is to write down what you think are the obstacles that may be keeping you back. For example, you are trying to find the right job, and every time you apply, you get turned down. You must look within yourself to find out why. Clear out the obstacles first, before you program your mind for success, or those obstacles will keep coming back to stop you.

If you can't do it yourself, have someone help you. Sometimes a therapist or close friend can help get you to where you need to be.

## Rule 3: Use subconscious programming before going to bed

The reason it is important to work with programming methods and techniques before bedtime is that the methods will go into your subconscious mind while you sleep.

The mind and body are relaxing now, so it will be easier to work with the subconscious, as you are not adding constant inputs.

Now you know the rules, how do you go about programming the subconscious mind. There are a few methods that experts have used and work. I'll relay them here for you.

## Method 1#: Use Metaphors

The subconscious mind works with metaphors all the time, so why not use this method to engrain in your mind what you want to be programmed into it.

Some people use symbols like seeds to set the stage for programming. Others use airplanes, while others use trees.

## Want It! Speak It! It's Yours!

When you start your programming session it is advisable to use soft, relaxing music. This helps relax your body and mind even further. Once you have relaxed start the process by feeding your subconscious mind with the thoughts you want to be planted.

## Method 2#: See the Result

Whatever goal you wish to achieve, see it having been completed. Use images to see your result. Maybe you can see yourself getting an award for employee of the month or year. Or you can see a nameplate with your name on it, followed by the word "CEO."

How does the image make you feel? Focus on this. What do you see and hear around you? Do you see colors? Do you hear other people talking? What do they say? Where are you exactly? Instead of the image, you can use video to see it. The choice of media is up to you.

## Method 3#: Bring up good memories

Sometimes, what can help with the process is by recalling a good memory of something you like and use it as an anchor to reconnect with your subconscious mind.

Try these methods and see how they work for you. You don't have to use all the methods. You can use one method one day and another method another day. Just make sure to use a method each day.

You'll be surprised by the results.

## Points to Ponder

These are questions you won't be graded on or required to answer. They are here simply for reflection and help you to remember more of what you read.

1. What have you learned from this step?
2. Have you tried the methods listed here in the past? If so, how did it work?
3. What method do you think may work best for you?

## [Step Three]

# How to Understand Dreams and Let Them Work for You

Dream. We all do it. Dreams can be entertaining, fun, romantic, disturbing, frightening, and even bizarre. Dreaming can occur during the day, as daydreaming, or at night. Regardless of when you dream, your subconscious processes what you have learned or obtained beforehand.

Dreaming is the way our subconscious processes inputs we receive from our senses. These processes are presented as stories or images. When you sleep, your conscious mind sleeps, but your subconscious mind doesn't. During this state, your subconscious mind processes, bringing up what was processed as images. The best way to explain this is by using an example. Let's say you were told of a problem that needed solving. You went to bed. Your subconscious mind will show it to you while you sleep.

## Want It! Speak It! It's Yours!

You may dream something, but let it go and forget about it. When asked what you dreamt about, you say that it was just a dream. But is it? Dreams occur for various reasons:

1. To display unconscious desires
2. To interpret signals our brain receives
3. To process information received
4. To work at therapy

Dreams are really a way for your subconscious mind to connect with God or the Universe, whoever you refer to as your higher power. A further way to state it is that dreams connect with your emotions and experiences for that day or life in general. They can contain themes, concerns, dream figures, objects, and more. Every aspect of the dream relates to the person's waking life. The question is figuring out what the dream means. That brings up this interesting question - Do you pay attention to what your dreams are telling you?

Want It! Speak It! It's Yours!

Dreams are there for two reasons: 1) to process information, 2) to provide a visual message. What do these reasons mean? Let's look at each one individually.

## 1. Process Information

When the brain processes information, it considers inputs from all the senses. It has been known, based on studies, that dreams help people learn about their feelings, beliefs, and values. The images and symbols in dreams have meaning based on those feelings, beliefs, and values of that person.

Dream experts have stated that the best way to analyze a dream is to look at each part of the dream as a separate entity and then bring all parts together. In other words, analyze each part of the dream and then combine each analysis into one analysis. This way, the dream can be better interpreted.

## 2. Provide a Visual Message

As stated in the previous paragraph, when you dream, those dreams contain images and symbols. Trying to figure out what those images and symbols mean, is the way to understand the dream.

For example, let's say you dream of flying. An image in your dream shows you flying. What does this mean? Flying dreams have been known to reflect a person's happy state. It means you have high hopes for yourself and your future.

Another example, which many dreamers have related is having sex. In some cases, the person in the dream may not be anyone you know. If so, this may be a wish fulfillment you want. The idea of sex isn't always what the vision or image is telling you. In some cases, dreaming of sex is more psychological. It could be telling you to merge contrasting aspects of yourself with your dream sex partner. In some cases, it can mean you are exploring your own needs and desire. You may not have a relationship in your life, so dreaming about sex is a way to release your frustration.

Do you see what I mean? The main point is that when you dream, you do so because of what you experienced at some point during that day or previous days.

Want It! Speak It! It's Yours!

## What Actions Do You Take?

Now you know the scientific reasons for dreaming and why you dream, is here an even more interesting question. Do you take any actions based on what you have dreamed? You may remember your dream in total recall. You could even write down your dream on paper and remember it to the finest detail. But, do you act on what you know?

You may know and understand your dream, but each image or symbol in your dream is reflecting on you. It is providing the information you need to know, so you can perhaps alter your steps or better understand a situation. Your subconscious mind is telling you, through images in your dream, that you must deal with the issue and solve it, especially if it is a problem.

So here is your challenge. When you dream of something you have been really focused on doing, or a goal you wish to achieve, take time to understand what those images and symbols mean. Piece the dream together based on those images and conclude as to what the dream is telling you. This is the first step in dream solving. I'll bet when you have done this; you will get the reason for the dream. Once you take necessary action, you'll see the results before your eyes, after which you'll go back to your dream, and say to yourself you did it. Your dream leads you to your goal.

Many rich and successful people became that way, because of what they dreamt. One inventor claimed he saw the entire invention in his head. He wrote it down as soon as he was able, and then acted on it. It took about a year, but he not only got a patent for his invention, but he also found a distributor. Today, he's a millionaire.

Here's another example. This guy, call him John Doe, graduated from business school. He really understands business development. One night, he dreamt of starting a business. He really loved math and finance. One day, he acted based on his dream and within a year, he started his first financial analysis consulting firm. He did so well with the business; he later went on to start and sell seven more businesses.

## What Will You Do?

The question is what you will do? Will you just be a dreamer and let it go, or will you take time to learn about your dream, and then follow it. Those people who don't pay attention to their dreams, end up losing on the chance they could have done great things.

Look at two good examples of people who didn't fail to act on their dreams. Anthony Robbins. He's one of the best self-help gurus today. He was very poor. His family broke up and divorced when he was a toddler. One day he had a dream of being a successful self-help coach. He didn't take that dream for granted. He borrowed some money and sent to work to change his life. Now, look at him.

What about T. Harv Eker. He was broke growing up. His family didn't have much. After graduating from college, he had a dream of opening a health and fitness store. He did. He went on to start one, but a few of them. He sold the businesses and made millions from the sell. He took what he learned and opened a school to help others do what he did. He acted on his dream.

## Dreams Do Come True

You may not believe this, but dreams do come true. You must believe they will. If you dream something good, and it is firmly anchored in your heart, and you follow it with a passion, you will achieve it. If you ignore it, you'll discover what could have been, won't be there for you.

Let no one tell you differently. Dreams will come true for you if you let them. Once you understand what your dream is about, take all the steps you need to achieve that which you dreamt. For example, if you dreamed you were driving a new car in a city you were never at before, take the dream apart and analyze each part separately. Write down the make, model, and color of the car, if you remember it. Write down what city you were in, if possible. Once you understand what the dream means, act on it. If you have a full-time job, look for that car. Research it if you must. Then look for the city. By doing the research, you'll soon discover your dream wasn't just a dream. It was a symbol telling you your life would change for the better.

Remember, this. You have dreams for a reason. Take advantage of the opportunity they provide when you have them. Don't dismiss them, unless they are bad ones. You may find that by acting on a dream, it may take you down a path to a successful career.

Want It! Speak It! It's Yours!

## Points to Ponder

These are questions you won't be graded on or required to answer. They are here simply for reflection and help you to remember more of what you read.

1. Do you better understand how dreams can work on your behalf?

2. What are dreams and why do you have them?

3. Have any good dreams lately?

## [Step Four]

## Learn How to Use Thought So It Will Take You Where You Want to Go.

Do you want it! Do you want to be successful in life? It all starts with a thought. To have the dreams you want, and to fulfill them, you need to put into your subconscious the thoughts that will get you there.

You may not believe this, but your thoughts can make you rich. Look at those who are rich. They fed their mind with the right thoughts. Their subconscious processed those thoughts and formed them into a dream. Then they recorded that dream and took the necessary step to make it happen.

How can you do this? I don't know if you are aware of this. Many of those who are prosperous do know it and practice it. What is this I am speaking about? It is a universal law. The law of vibration. I did not mention this earlier, but one thing you need to understand about the brain is that it's made of neurons. Each neuron releases a chemical that turns into electrical impulses. What do you think the EEG machine picks up when it is connected to your brain?

Energy vibrates at a frequency. This is electronics 101. Every time we think, or use our subconscious mind, we are creating energy that vibrates at a certain frequency. When that frequency matches a frequency in the universe, you receive whatever is vibrating at the frequency. It's like when you pick up the phone. You make a call. Frequency is created by those buttons you push. The frequency travels over phone lines until it reaches a phone that has a receiver vibrating at that same frequency. When that happens, a signal is sent to sound an alarm. Thusly, you hear your phone ring.

How does this relate to getting what you want? If you feed your mind with the right thoughts, your subconscious mind will provide you with the right results. You could learn what you need to know by way of dreaming it, or you will receive a sign.

## Want It! Speak It! It's Yours!

What matters here is that you need to want it first. If you want it, you will feed your subconscious mind with the right thoughts. These thoughts will work on you while you sleep and give you what you want. Or, you will find the right way to accomplish what you are looking for.

What does the law of vibration, the subconscious mind, and dreams have anything to do with what we can achieve or want in our lives? Let's put it this way. Without thinking the right thoughts, your subconscious mind won't receive the right inputs. Without the right inputs, your subconscious mind can't guide you, whether it is by dreaming or by simply point you in the right direction. You have various avenues at your disposal to help you get what you want. It's up to you to use them. But to use them, you must start it out with thought, or want.

If you want something, what do you do? Do you go after it, or do you wait and hope someone gives it to you? I hope the answer is you go after it. This is what I am speaking about. A guy named John Assaraf spoke of people like a magnet. You will attract what you want to you. You must believe you will achieve what you want and the universe will open to you.

Want It! Speak It! It's Yours!

The reason people don't get what they want is that they really don't want it. They think they won't get it, so why bother. This is a self-defeating attitude, but one that many people seem to have.

## Don't let this happen to you.

Keep this in your mind. One thought created the Universe. One thought created the earth. Everything around us was created with one thought. You can create everything around you with one thought as well.

## Points to Ponder

These are questions you won't be graded on or required to answer. They are here simply for reflection and help you to remember more of what you read.

1. Do you understand to be successful in life, it all starts with a thought?

2. Do you believe that thoughts create energy?

3. What are you thinking about what now?

## [Step Five]

## Understand How Your Feelings Can Control Thoughts for Good or Bad

Do you know that feelings can direct the way you react to things in your life? Yes, feelings do have a play. Whether you know it or not the way you feel can have a direct bearing on what you think. If you think happy thoughts, you feel good. If you think bad thoughts, you feel bad. So, if you monitor your feelings, you can monitor your thoughts since thoughts produce feelings.

Someone once told me to monitor your feelings, as this will be a way to know what you are thinking. Why is this true? Because your thoughts vibrate at a certain frequency and that frequency controls your emotional state. If you are feeling bad, you are vibrating at a frequency that'll trigger bad feelings or emotions. The same is true for good thoughts.

## Want It! Speak It! It's Yours!

A good example of this is when you wake up from a bad dream. You feel bad because your nightmare produced negative feelings in you. You'll have these feelings all day, as they are in your subconscious mind. How can you overcome these feelings? The best way is to shift your feelings and your mental state. When you do this, your positive feelings will change how your subconscious mind takes it in and processes it. You'll feel better and begin attracting more good feelings.

One great way to change your state and vibrate at the right energy is by allowing one key element to take control. What is that element? Love. That's right. Love is the answer. Depending on who you talk to, there are those who believe that love is the most powerful feeling there is.

If you are having a bad day, or you woke up in that state, turn your feelings around. The right thoughts will help in your road to success.

Want It! Speak It! It's Yours!

## Points to Ponder

These are questions you won't be graded on or required to answer. They are here simply for reflection and help you to remember more of what you read.

1. Did you know that feelings can decide what type of thoughts your subconscious receives?

2. Do you understand that if you feel a certain way, you can change your feelings?

3. You may not understand this at first, but the attribute love does and will take you far. Do you believe that?

## [Step Six]

# By Speaking with Power and Conviction You'll Go Far and Be Successful

How can you dictate what your subconscious mind will accept? As I covered already, the subconscious mind works with inputs from the five senses. The main input is thought.

Thoughts can be absorbed by what you read, speak, or hear. If you read good, up building words, it will help you in your endeavors to be successful. If you write, the words you use will have an impact on your future. So, you need to make sure your words are in alignment with what you want to achieve. The last way is through hearing. What you hear does get processed by the subconscious. As such, listening to the right words from others, what is spoken on TV or radio, or even the Internet, can affect your future outcomes.

# Want It! Speak It! It's Yours!

Of all the ways I mentioned, let's look at speaking. The words you use can have an influence what you recall later. What can you speak that will be in harmony with your future visions and goals? You can speak of your vision daily. You can even talk about the dream you had if it relates to your goal. For instance, you can tell others what you dreamt. You can let your friends and family know your daily vision for your future. The more you speak of it, the stronger it becomes. Your subconscious mind can absorb what you say, each time you say it, thereby increasing the emphasis on it.

Remember the adage of how do you get to Carnegie Hall? You must practice, practice, and practice again. The same goes with speaking. The more you speak, the more your subconscious will take it in and perform the duties necessary to achieve what you want.

Listen to famous speakers. How do they relate their goals and visions? They mention them when speaking. But when they do it, they use powerful words. The words used are persuasive and mean something. Therefore, when you speak, you need to know the words you are using. Make every word a power word. Not only will these words attract attention, but your subconscious mind will pick up on it too.

## Want It! Speak It! It's Yours!

When you do speak, believe the words you use. Like I said in the previous paragraph, every word needs to mean something. But if you don't believe in what you are saying, it has no power behind it. They are just meaningless words. You must believe what you are saying for the words to hold power.

When speaking about words, are we talking about speaking in public? Not necessarily. When speaking, I am focused on more speaking affirmations. By speaking affirmations, you are training your subconscious mind to accept what you say as real.

The best way to produce the results you want is by repeating affirmations daily. Such a technique will build your psyche, but it will also keep you in the mindset of succeeding.

It doesn't take long. Even ten minutes will help greatly. You start doing this using mediation. When a person meditates, many things happen from a physical and mental standpoint. We put our focus on the internal side of our bodies. When we do this, we shut out the outside world. It is like being in a state of sleep, but you don't lose consciousness.

When we reach a certain level of meditation (alpha and theta), our brain becomes more stable and develop stronger frequencies. What we are doing is reaching the subconscious mind so that we can control it.

According to those who practice meditation, when meditating, the person is entering a stage where they have a higher level of intuitive sense. At this state, the person can develop creative thoughts and can program the subconscious.

## Points to Ponder

These are questions you won't be graded on or required to answer. They are here simply for reflection and help you to remember more of what you read.

1. Do you practice affirmations?
2. Do you know what words have power behind them?
3. you know any famous speakers?

Want It! Speak It! It's Yours!

## [Step Seven]

# How to Believe in Yourself to Achieve What You Want in Life

The key to being successful is thinking about what you want and going for it. However, there is one obstacle in the way of getting there. This is having a belief in yourself. If you don't believe in your own talents and abilities, you won't make it. You must keep telling yourself how important it is to believe in yourself. If you truly do, your dreams will come true.

What about all the investors in history? If they didn't believe in themselves, we wouldn't have the inventions today like TV, the radio, computers, etc. We'd been in the dark if it weren't for Thomas Edison. Study people from the past, particularly those who succeeded in something like inventing. If you read deeply enough, you may find they had a lot of belief in themselves. This is something you must do likewise.

## Want It! Speak It! It's Yours!

If you find it hard to do so, seek help. Find someone you know and trust to help you get there. Getting help from someone, who has lived it and knew the hurdles, can help you too. Don't be afraid to seek advice about how to develop a belief in yourself, if you don't have it already.

One good way to help you with your belief systems is by meditation. When you go into meditation, you can repeat certain phrases or affirmations, that can help you focus on your belief systems. These affirmations can be words or phrases that can go into your subconscious mind and help trigger those moments when you need a belief in yourself.

Meditation is a time when you can think positive about yourself and your situation. If you are struggling with deciding about a job prospect, by meditating, you are asking your subconscious to give you answers. If you feed your mind with the right thoughts earlier, your subconscious mind will respond.

Want It! Speak It! It's Yours!

## Points to Ponder

These are questions you won't be graded on or required to answer. They are here simply for reflection and help you to remember more of what you read.

1. What is one way to believe in yourself?

2. Do you practice meditation?

3. What affirmations do you use on yourself?

## [Step Eight]

# Use Three Methods to Achieve What You Want and Succeed

Gurus would say if you want success in your life, you must follow three methods. If these three methods are followed correctly and on point, you will achieve what you seek out or want.

1. Ask for what you want. It's that simple. Simply state it or write it down. Then affirm it in your mind. Your subconscious mind will process it and help to make it happen. Just make sure you are clear as to what you want. You can't have any doubts about yourself because if you are, the procedure won't work.

2. Believe. If you really want something, you need to believe. I touched on this earlier in this chapter. The reason I am repeating it here is that it is so necessary part of the procedure. If it weren't I would have just

moved on to other ideas. However, since I did cover it in some detail in this chapter, I won't bother you with many details. What I will say is believing in yourself is a must if you want to succeed in your life.

3. Receive. This sounds so simple, doesn't it? You may not realize this, but there are people, many people in fact, who don't know how to receive things in their lives. If someone gives the person a gift, the person receiving the gift feels bad. It's hard to understand why. Perhaps, the person feels guilty for taking something, if the gift wasn't earned.

By learning to receive, you'll find just how abundant your life can be. It doesn't take much thought. Just open your hands and your heart to it, and what you want will come to you. If you feel good about what you are getting, you are increasing the chance of receiving it. The universe will make sure you get what you want.

Jesus said it best at Matthew 21:22 when he said, "Whatsoever ye shall ask in prayer, believing, ye shall receive." Even Mark stated in Mark 11:24 that, "What things soever ye desire, when ye pray, believe that ye receive them, and ye shall have them." This can happen to you as well, if only you believe and act.

There you have it. The formula for success. Without these three methods, your chances of succeeding in life won't matter. You may get where you want to be, but without the proper direction, your success could be short-lived.

## Points to Ponder

These are questions you won't be graded on or required to answer. They are here simply for reflection and help you to remember more of what you read.

1. Do you know what it means to ask what you want?
2. Do you know what having a belief in yourself means?
3. Have you ever received anything from a stranger and accepted it or did you reject it?

## [Step Nine]

# Use This Method to Help You Accomplish Your Goals and Become Successful

So far you have been instructed on how to use the subconscious mind to get what you want.

It all starts with a thought. Speaking will help reinforce your subconscious thoughts by using affirmations. There is another strategy you can use that will help reinforce your goals and future. This is by writing your thoughts down.

There are various ways to write what you wish to accomplish for yourself. I'll cover each part below:

1. Make a clear, detailed plan: What better way than to be focused on what you wish to achieve for your future than to have a plan. Write it down so it can become concrete. Your plan needs to be a clear

strategy. If you need it to be in steps, so be it. Just as long as you create it.

2. Write a business plan: If you don't know how to write one, research it. There are many samples and examples online. There are books on writing a business plan. There is also software you can get to help you create one. A business plan will list everything you plan on doing and the steps you will take to get there to start your business or create the income you want.

Whatever you decide to do, take your approach one step at a time. As you progress forward, do not be overwhelmed by what you need to do. Everyone, who succeeded in life, went about what you will need to do the same way. So, you are not alone. Remember that.

If you need help from others, do so. Get any help you need. Sometimes, some decisions must be made that require careful planning and thought. Don't be afraid to reach out if you find yourself stuck, or are not sure what procedure to follow next. Keep in mind the most successful and famous people wrote down their thoughts and goals. By getting into

## Want It! Speak It! It's Yours!

the habit of writing down your thoughts and goals, it will help lead you to become a success yourself.

Here is an example of what I mean. I remember reading about a man, who as a teenager, wanted to become the leader of his country – a prime minister.

But not just a prime minister, but a famous one.

Every day this young man would write in a journal how he felt about it. One such quote was, "I must become a great man."

It is because he wrote this down every day in his journal, these words were pressed on his subconscious mind so much, that he took the appropriate steps to achieve that which he wanted. Yes, he ended up becoming a famous prime minister.

Researchers who have studied what makes people successful have discovered that writing down goals and ideas is very common among those who later become successful. It appears that the more you write down your thoughts and goals for your future, it stimulates your brain to achieve the success you want.

Want It! Speak It! It's Yours!

However, no matter what you write about, there is one important step you need to take to make sure it all happens. This step will be explained next.

## [Step Ten]

# What You Need to Know to Take the Big Step

Are you ready? Want to know what the big step is? Without this step, you'll end up going nowhere. You can do all the previous steps, but without doing this step, the likelihood of you reaching your goals will be slim.

What is this big step? Drumroll, please....

## *Taking Action!*

That's right. If you want to reach the finish line, you need to take action. Why take action? You may think that the subconscious mind will do everything for you. Guide you. I hate to say this, but the subconscious mind will guide you by giving you answers as to what you will need to do, but the result is taking action.

Wishing won't do anything. Hoping won't do anything. No matter how much you feed your mind with good thoughts, regarding your goals and plans, without taking action towards them, it'll be like wasted energy.

Let's consider an example. How about America's favorite past time, baseball. You could have the best team on the field. But, if they can't hit the ball safely someplace, the team won't win. Also, it would be good if they had a good pitcher to keep the other team from scoring.

This is exactly how the game of life is played. If you think up great ideas how to make money, but you don't capitalize on the ideas, you won't go anywhere. On the other hand, if you do take a step forward, you are on your way to reaching what you set out to do.

If you sit in a chair, think about what you want to happen, get the thought into your subconscious mind, then you put feelings into it, then you act on what you thought, you will reach the plateau and achieve your dream or thought. That is what it is all about.

The old saying, "actions speak louder than words" is all so true. It fits perfectly with the laws of the Universe. If you connect action to all the laws of the Universe, you will find

## Want It! Speak It! It's Yours!

there will be more harmony, love, peace, contentment, and joy in the world.

Unfortunately, the world itself does not have this but you can if you put forth the effort to. All it takes is one thought on your part and then you just process that thought with your feelings. Then you in turn act on that thought and the rest will come about. The Universe will open itself up and pour down upon you your heart's desire. And all you had to do was think, feel, and act on it.

If you remember to take action, you can gain for yourself riches, glory, power, or whatever you want to achieve. This is your life. You choose the direction you want to go.

You may or may not recall, but I spoke of the mind like a magnet. When you use your subconscious mind, you are acting like a magnet, attracting to you whatever frequency your subconscious is connecting with.

Here's something to bite into. By taking action, you are using the energy you created when you used though, for whatever endeavor it may be. In a sense, you are completing a circuit. You are connected to the universe. When this happens, your mind (magnet) will attract whatever you are thinking about.

In a sense, your subconscious mind will act as the sender and the universe as the receiver. You will be attracted to whatever frequency your magnet builds. However, to complete the circuit and have that magnet work in your favor, you need to take action. Electricity doesn't flow unless it has something to push it forward in the circuit (amps). When the amp takes action, electricity flows.

## Points to Ponder

These are questions you won't be graded on or required to answer. They are here simply for reflection and help you to remember more of what you read.

1. What is the biggest step you need to take for your life to work for you?

2. Why are actions necessary for your thoughts to work correctly?

3. Taking action is like completing an electrical circuit. Why is that?

## [Step Eleven]

# Taking Action Means Doing This One Thing

In the previous step, I mentioned taking action. If you are to fulfill any lifelong dream or future you have planned, you must also do this as well, or take action won't take you far.

What is it? Being in motion. What does this mean? Being in motion means doing something that will allow you to succeed in the action steps you take. No matter what course you pursue, to reach it, you must take action. Action requires you to be in motion to get it done.

But I thought taking action meant literally doing something? Yes and no. Taking action means you begin the race, but being in motion is when you run. For instance, if you want to run water, you take action by grabbing the faucet. But when you are in motion, you turn the faucet. Do you understand the concept of being in motion now?

How can you achieve success in your life, especially in business? You must take steps to build your network and build your brand.

## Build Your Network

Set things in motion by contacting those who can help you get to the position you need be. These people can be a business owner or future clients. They can also be friends and family members.

Surround yourself with people, who can help advance your career. For example, you can connect with a lawyer, accountant, sales person, marketing person, etc. The people you associate with would be people, who know you and know the industry you want to get into. The more you know them, the easier it will be to get the help you need to start your business.

When you associate with the right people, suddenly, you will notice a change in the way your life works. Now, your daily life will change and lead you in a different direction that you are not accustomed to. But this is good as it allows you to alter your life but in a good way. You'll start seeing your dreams come true and will be happier as a result. If you don't change, you won't succeed. That is the point.

## Build Your Brand

To do well, you need to build a brand, so people will know and do business with you. It's easier to start and build a business if you specialize in an area or niche. For example, if you are the only one who knows how to make an apple pie without the added ingredients, so it still tastes good, you have created a niche, and will do well.

The question is how you can become recognizes?

How do you build a client or customer base? Let's define what branding is. In a nutshell, branding is how people see you. If someone was approached by a person and was asked who makes the best apple pie, and you know that person is you, you have built up your brand.

Branding is a way to establish values and characteristics for a certain product or service. Everyone associates Big Macs with McDonald's. It's the branding.

Branding is when you are in control. Without it, you won't establish a successful career. It can be considered a statement that helps you make personal and professional decisions. It also helps people understand you and what you offer. This includes what you value and what level and quality of work you will provide.

Despite the fact, branding helps build a customer base, remember one fact. It isn't about landing any client. It's about aiming for and obtaining only the clients, who want to work with you or buy your product. They are interested in what you offer, and only want to do business with you.

## So how do you go about building your brand?

1. It starts with knowing your brand. The best way to know your brand is to know what people think of you.

   Here's a great way to find out. Write down the values people, you associate with, or have had contact with, would use to describe you and the business you are trying to start or are engaged with.

## Want It! Speak It! It's Yours!

Make sure to use words that are honest, positive, and authentic.

2. As I said in an earlier paragraph, for this step, you need to specialize in something. When you know what you want, be vocal about it. This will help you stand out. Think what you bring to the table no one else does.

3. When you start your business, it may be a great idea to create a bio of yourself. By creating one, it will help advertise who you are. You can use it to spread the word about your business online and when networking. When creating your bio include your education, work experience, any published writing, press releases, awards you've received, volunteer work, and even your personal interests. Your bio will be able for the world to see.

4. A great way to build your brand is by blogging. It seems many people are blogging. You can talk about whatever you wish. You can showcase your creativity and how you manage your business as a leader. When people read your blog, they will get a

clear idea of who you are. They may also be able to contact you at some point.

5. Use social media. There are various social sites you can join. For professionals, LinkedIn is the biggest one. With LinkedIn, you can promote yourself and your business. You can create a profile, where you list your work experiences if you have any, academics, and achievements.

If you look at it this way, it can be considered your digital resume. You can use the bio you created under point number three above.

You can use Facebook. Although Facebook is more for social connections, some people use it for spreading their businesses online. They set up a company page and advertise their businesses that way. You can also do this if you wish. The main thing about Facebook is you are exposing yourself to the world, but not in a business sort of way. However, you can set up your privacy settings so only your immediate friends, you connect with will be able to reach you.

Want It! Speak It! It's Yours!

Twitter is another social site you may take advantage of. You can spread the word about your business by using this social site. Millions of people are subscribed to it. Think of all the people you may know, or can connect with. These people can retweet whatever you tweet, especially if it is good.

There are so many social sites; you need to research them. Be careful with some. There are those who are unscrupulous.

I just covered the key step you need to take to be successful. While letting your subconscious mind guide your step, you must put forth the effort to take action and then put your plan in motion.

If you complete all the steps, you will have only set yourself. Don't let that happen to you.

## Points to Ponder

These are questions you won't be graded on or required to answer. They are here simply for reflection and help you to remember more of what you read.

## Want It! Speak It! It's Yours!

1. Taking action means doing this one thing. What is it?

2. You must build two things for your life to work right. One is to build your network. What is the other one?

3. What is one way to build your brand?

## [Step Twelve]

# Take the Mentality that It's Yours and Let No One Say Differently

Guess what? You have reached the pentacle. You got here. Can you see your dreams coming true? Can you see everything happening to you that is supposed to happen? If you don't see your dreams coming true yet, don't despair. You will see your dreams come true. In fact, if you haven't seen any results yet, this should inspire you to push forward and keep up with the steps you learned in this book.

Sometimes, things take a bit of time to work. That's just how the universe works. However, with patience and perseverance, you will see the light at the end of the tunnel. The steps in this book worked for Alex, the woman you read about in the introduction. At the end of this book, I'll give details as to how she's doing. Just don't give up.

## Want It! Speak It! It's Yours!

Just keep in your subconscious that the plan is working. Always think that the plan works. If you work hard and stay on track, your efforts will not be in vain. Your strategies are being complete.

The next step is to build your empire. Don't be lackadaisical about it. Once you have your empire built, keep building on your success. Don't fall into mediocrity. Always think of a way to capitalize on your current business. Keep reaching new heights. Develop a following and build it. Work to make sure those who follow you, believe in you and your product.

Just don't quit. Allow others to help you along. If you feel pinched or under pressure, take a break and meditate. This will help you get centered. But above all things, do not forsake working each step in this book. Each step was put there for a reason. If you skip any step, you will fail to achieve what you want.

Isn't the reason you read this book was to learn how you can change your life and aim it in the way you really want it. Be prosperous and happy, knowing you have made it to the top. You can't get there until you do the steps.

## Want It! Speak It! It's Yours!

Just like alcoholics can't get to that level of sobriety unless they follow all the steps required by AA. The same goes with every one of you, who are reading this book. You can't skip a step, or you won't be able to run the course you were met too.

Think of it this way. For an electrical circuit to work, there needs to be a complete circuit. The wire must travel from negative to positive. All components that go into the circuit must be wired to it. If one component is missing, the circuit will not work.

Remember all that I said in the above few paragraphs, and make sure you complete them. If you must, have someone work with you. Don't try to do it alone, if you feel the need to have someone help you.

The world is your oyster if you want it. You must believe in yourself, and put forth the motion to get it done. The universe will open a way for you if you take the steps required to make your life work.

Proceed to the next page for some important information.

## Points to Ponder

These are questions you won't be graded on or required to answer. They are here simply for reflection and help you to remember more of what you read.

1. Are you ready to take on the world?

2. Have you completed each step in this book faithfully?

3. Have you completed your journey to creating your own business?

Want It! Speak It! It's Yours!

# Getting What You Want by Making Sacrifices

With all this talk about getting what you want and using thought to get it, do you know to accomplish great things, some times sacrifices must be made? It is true. I have known people, who gave up their social lives just to finish college. They knew how important getting a good education would mean for them and their future.

For those of you who went to college, you saw the dramatic difference in your lives from being at home with your parents, and going to high school. Once you started college, you had to do most of the work yourself, especially if the college you attended was far from home.

What about those of you who are working? After college, you landed a job you liked and started working there. You advanced yourself. It took a lot of sacrificing to get there.

## Want It! Speak It! It's Yours!

What I am trying to get here is that sacrifices are usually and often made for a person to proceed from step one to step two, or step two to step three. No matter what sacrifices you make, to make your life work, you must stay focused on your goals and aspirations, or you could lose out on where you want to be.

Someone told me one time that it is easier to lose oneself and one's focus. It no doubt will be hard work to get focused and stay there, and it probably will take a great deal of sacrificing on your part to get there, but once you have arrived, you'll take a step back, and realize that it was all worth it.

Want It! Speak It! It's Yours!

## Are You Prepared for What You Want?

Think back a second and let what you just read sink in. What is it you really want in life? What do you want to achieve? If you have a desire in mine, the first step is by thinking about that desire strongly. Let it sink in your subconscious mind. Then wait one night for your subconscious mind to show you what will happen if you pursue it. Your answer will come in the form of a dream or a sign.

Remember what I stated earlier about frequency? Your thoughts create energy that vibrates at a certain frequency. When you use your subconscious mind, your mind is vibrating at that frequency. As such, the universe will match that frequency, resulting in what you want.

You may ask if I can use my mind to create wealth? I say yes you can. Think about the job you want, if you are looking. If you have a job but want a promotion, think about it. Whatever method you want to obtain wealth, think about it. The thoughts you create, or the thoughts someone, who talked to you about it, went into your subconscious mind. By this happening, the subconscious mind produces the right frequency, which in turn opens a way for you to gain that wealth, be it a new job or promotion.

The key to getting anything you want in life is by your belief system. If your beliefs are centered on making money or living in abundance, you will become successful in life. On the other hand, if your beliefs are limited or based on insecurities, you won't get what you want. If you were brought up to believe you should live in poverty, because that is all you know, you would continue to live that way. So how can you change your beliefs?

You are your own creator. You get to decide how your life will unfold. Many practitioners state that if you follow those who have lived an exemplary life, you will find they had a strong belief system and knew what it took to live in abundance. They practiced this every day. To be successful, you follow their lead. By doing exactly what they did to be successful, you can repeat this process and become successful yourself.

## Wrap Up

Remember Alex from the introduction? Well, I just wanted to let you know that she went through each step in this book, and completed each one. The result was amazing.

She has accomplished her dream of becoming an Entrepreneur. She now owns a restaurant and is doing extremely well. Why did she get this far?

Because of these three famous words: She

*wanted it!*

*She Spoke it!*

*It's Her's!*

If she can do it, so can you. Use her as an example of what you can do. It doesn't matter what business you want to start. If it is in your heart to do it, go for it. You just must want it, declare it, and desire it. If you do all these things, I can guarantee it will be yours.

## Want It! Speak It! It's Yours!

As stated earlier in this book, believe in yourself and you can accomplish a great deal.

www.ingramcontent.com/pod-product-compliance
Lightning Source LLC
Chambersburg PA
CBHW050016230526
45470CB00003B/987